A Deluge of Darkness

Valentina
Montenegro-Venero

BookLeaf Publishing

India | USA | UK

Presentation by *BookLeaf Publishing*

Web: www.bookleafpub.com

E-mail: info@bookleafpub.com

ISBN: 9789360949303

First edition 2024

To the darkness we all must face, and the strength that it highlights within us. To those of you struggling with the dark, that you may leave it stronger than ever before, so that you can one day see its beauty. To the bright side.

ACKNOWLEDGEMENT

I would like to thank my parents for supporting me in writing this book, and always listening to my poetry, which I wrote anywhere I could. I would also like to thank my grandmother, who evidently passed on her love of writing poetry to me. I would like to thank all the great poets for providing inspiration for me and beautiful words for the world to read. I am thankful for all my teachers who helped enhance my writing skills, and for the situations, good and bad, that led to me writing this collection. Because, though the situations were not always positive ones, without them, I would not have ended up where I am today. I most certainly would not be publishing this collection right now. Thank you to Book Leaf Publishing for publishing A Deluge of Darkness, which plays such a large role in this new chapter of my life. Lastly, I would like to thank my readers. Thank you for giving my poetry a chance, whether it left a mark on you or not. I am grateful to each and every person for reading this collection that is so close to my heart, and really hope that you found some value in it, or at the very least, comfort in knowing that you are not alone.

PREFACE

I have been writing poetry on and off for years, but did not start taking it seriously until summer of 2023, when I did a two-week summer program at the University of Oxford in Creative Writing. After the program ended, I continued writing poetry on my own, and ended up writing these, along with many others. The title of this book came to me while I was writing its content. Prior to deciding this would even become a book, I was writing poems, and noticed they were quite dark. Perhaps this is because, in my opinion, some of the best poems ever written, and the most famous, are centered around dark themes. This is not to say that I do not write poems of love and beauty, but only that I decided that for my first published poetry collection, I wanted to follow the theme of darkness. Some of these poems are quite dark, and that should be noted before going into them, but many have a bright side. Though I wrote some of these by putting myself inside someone else's shoes, others are composed of my emotions, thoughts, and experiences. There was a period where I was in a dark place myself, but I got past it, so if you are in a similar situation, do not lose hope. And most importantly, remember that you are not alone. I sought to humanize processes that everybody goes through in life, and not only provide the dark side, but the bright side too, because both are ever present. I hope you enjoy A Deluge of Darkness, and that these poems may inspire you to write your own stories.

Allured by the Dark

The allure of darkness must have something to
do
With the itch we all feel to let danger through
Your nerves tingle; anticipation and fear
But that is not all; this feels sincere.

You feel more alive than you've in a longtime
And you needed not even to drink any wine
For danger is so insanely primordial
Your body can sense it; it is corporeal.

You hate it yet love it; you cannot decide
If you should stay in place or run back inside
Such is the mystique of what we do not know
There are two kinds of people; those who stay or
who go.

Exile

I lie here, all alone,
Watching, waiting for the snow.
The snow that destroys,
The snow that falls gracefully,
The snow that harms those who are too friendly.
Perfect beauty with perfect aim,
Never missing, unforgiving.
He stood up, stared in space,
An exiled man with no face.
Awaking with a start, I steady myself,
A reminder I am here; I reinvented myself.
Gone-extinct are the days,
The ones I long for most.
I idolized ideas that I idolize no more.
Man or battle warrior, the second was a must.
I wasn't weak; I got accused of having cheek.
So, as I lie here, my heart battering,
I stand up, try to forsake my notoriety.
My mental-corslet secured in place,
I grab ahold of my light-bearer, just in case.
Striding forward, reaching for the doorknob,
Throwing myself outside, I find out what I knew
not.
I see a figure, making good pace,
He seems to be wearing a collar made of lace.

Time unfreezes, my mind snaps back on,
I shout wildly as I close the door in fright.
The last thing I see, running for my life,
Is a decorated hand that claws out my face.
"Take me back," I whisper.
I needn't have spoken,
For, no matter where I ran,
My heart would always be broken.

Love is Akin to Pain

If love were not true
We would not survive
If pain were not true
We would not be alive
One is welcomed
The other despised
Except the former hurts more
Than the latter sometimes.

Peaceful Passing

5

I slide into Death's warm embrace
As midnight passes by
I had never known such comfort
As when I lay and die.

Melancholy

Melancholy hits like a wave in the abyss
It stands its ground and emits a low sound
Such a sound is felt in one's very core
'Twill make you wish to be spit onto shore
The beach provides but interim relief
To remain on it you must utterly believe
You possess strength the blue sea lacks
Watch it from afar, see the waves crash
Onto the sand, in a threatening manner
You could be next if you do not run faster
The waves will circle you, as predators do prey
Thou must not let the ocean drag thee down
Running towards the deep will not wish the
waves away
You must fight to stay on land, every single day.

Hope

The essence of hope is such that we
As humans could miss it for eternity
It evades the gallows where men go to die,
And the narrow bathroom stalls where others go
to cry.
But mostly, it evades those who question their
existence,
Those who wait for life to beg their forgiveness
For bringing them to earth, with no consent
given
Men, women and children by the million
If a little speck of hope was blown onto their
path
Perhaps they would not be so resigned and sad.

Time

The memories resurface
In the middle of the night
I remind myself they are my past
As I lie on my bed in fright
The past escapes, then returns
The present knows its place
What will happen when the future
Makes passing precious time a race?

Ode to Springtime

Would that I knew how springtime can resist
Returning to winter's piercing abyss
Its sorrow taints any who dare cross it
The beauty within hidden by casket.

Spring lies waiting, immune to nature's
Harsh surface. It is but that: solely the surface
Warmth and allure lie beneath the surface,
Never trust what you see on the surface.

You may well be one of the lucky few
Who revels in winter and sees it through
Frosty snowflakes, hail then rain
Flowers in bloom, skiing in may
Near opposite seasons shake hands in glee
Though all assume them to be enemies.

If you ask my opinion, spring alone
Sees winter's true self, not how it is shown
Spring's strength surpasses that of every season
And we all rely on its skill of completion.

For Death Loved Life

I am in love with life
Alas, I am Death
The very worst of anyone
Cannot love the very best.

The Garden of Death

You are a garden
That once was a flower
I admire your roses
Your lilies and posies
The thorns, especially
Are my most favorite
They remind me that treasure
Is never unwavering
But thorns remain
Through dusk and dawn
Embedded in the mind
Even when one is gone
Alive, you were my rose
But in death, you became more.

Composure

Thy pain is exposed
By grief
So composed — deadly.

Grief

Grief is the shadow of death
One follows the other in every sense
To split them up would be infeasible
Grief is not a process easily relievable
What shadow has grief?
Joy, some believe
The unlucky remain in desolation
All stemming from a potent connection
Grief is but love that some believe dies
But even when none are left
That love survives.

Writing by Fire

A candle aflame alights the dark night
And allows a mere poet to on paper write
Stronger it grows per the warmth it is fed
How long will this last? There is no way to tell
Malnourished as the flame becomes
It flickers thanks to failing lungs
No longer is the home well lit
As the fire throws a fit
Lines grow hard to read
As pupils and parchment struggle to meet
Even so, the pencil persists
Though a silky voice tells it to quit
The once begun pleasing poem
Made by fire to look golden
Is now a jungle of tangled words
Amid which once lay many a verse
But all contemplation suddenly ceases
When I notice the light is no longer breathing
Darkness engulfs my every sense
Could it be Death himself?
Nay, for Death in spite of his role
Would let me finish my poem before taking my
soul.

Death

O Death! Where are you now?
Partaking in frivolities with Eternity?
Or rescuing men in Life's stead?
Thou art everywhere — perfectly.

Misery

Simply nights away, I stare at the decay
Never before have I so desired to pray
Clinging to the last scrap of my rotting sanity
I recall how apathy was the result of my vanity.

Mercy is a kindness, one I will not be shown
Torture will bless me down to my bones
My icy skin licked by the flames
After all, what is this but a game?

They need not torment my body
Though they will anyhow if it makes them
happy
Misery is the friend of revenge
The latter spreads the former until the end.

After all, I must pay my due
Such is life; mine must end too.

A Ghost at Their Grave

I parse my epitaph with vexation
Sister, friend, daughter, lover of nations.
At no time was I a patriot
And my favorite plant was silver ragwort.

Though speaking ill of the dead is parlous
Our talk of the living is hardly proper
Carnations and daisies lie on my tomb
But my uncle's roses thrust out the gloom.

My favorite color was that of water
I revel seeing some worn in my honor
The victim of an echt eulogy
Though to my funeral went the whole
community.

After today, will I hear my name?
For the living, it seems, is reserved all the fame.

An Encounter With Death

When I was 12, I dreamed a dream
I'd had a caller in my sleep
A gentleman dressed in fine fabrics,
He had about him an air so tragic.

Intrigued, I was, so I asked his name
"Death," he replied inside my brain
How could that be so? Then I awoke
I knew 'twas not yet time to go.

To Forgive or Not

Forgiveness requires one vicious sin
Committed by someone you once let in
Though many opt to pardon their grievance
Fret not if you cannot yet relieve them
"Forgive! Forgive!" they preach
But 'tis too late to unearth the seed
Nay, the tree has already sprouted
The damage is done
Their hatred outed
Time does not heal every lesion
So forgive, or not, at your own leisure.

Carelessness

Danger persistent creates caution committed
Wariness engrains itself in your mind
When safety becomes scarce and unkind
But caution committed erases stories unwritten
And carelessness, though one should heed it
Remains there, staunchly, if only one should
need it.

Curiosity's Imagination

Stories in which one is not the subject
Carry Curiosity to which others are subject
And painting pictures of what could be
Is the closest to reality we will ever be.

A Deluge of Darkness

A deluge of darkness accompanies humanity
'Tis clear in darkened thoughts
And demonstrations of profanity
Crestfallen is Life
By reason of our strife
Is this amendable?
Or is it far too late?
Only we decide
Humanity's fate.

www.ingramcontent.com/pod-product-compliance
Lightning Source LLC
LaVergne TN
LVHW010848200726

843508LV00012B/2817

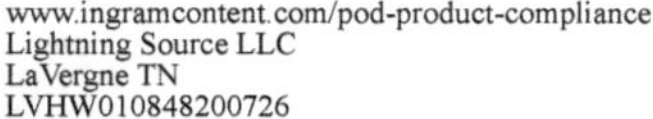